FENG SHUI
for the nursery

FENG SHUI
for the nursery

by Debra Keller
Edited by Kelli F. Giammarco
Illustrated by Mary Ross

ARIEL BOOKS

**Andrews McMeel
Publishing**
Kansas City

04 05 06 07 08 TWP 10 9 8 7 6 5 4 3 2 1

ISBN: 0-7407-4678-2

Library of Congress Catalog Card Number: 2004101543

FENG SHUI

for the nursery

Welcome to parenthood. Or perhaps you're just looking for some help in redecorating the nursery. Either way, you've come to the right place. Inside this book are lots of wonderful ideas about how to create a nursery environment that will help give your baby the best possible start in life.

No, we're not talking designer sheets and rocker-gliders with electric seat warmers. This book is about the important things: colors that influence mood, fabrics that encourage growth, symbols that inspire awareness, scents and sounds that soothe and calm. These are the cornerstones of nursery Feng Shui.

Simply put, Feng Shui is the ancient Chinese art of arranging an environment to influence one's life in positive ways. The words *Feng Shui* literally mean "wind and water"—two of the most vital life-giving elements on Earth. By applying the principles of Feng Shui to your nursery you can create a stimulating and enriching atmosphere that can help your baby grow up happy and fulfilled in body, mind, and spirit.

Feng Shui is based on the belief that everything on Earth is teeming with energy (called *chi)* and all energy seeks a state of balance. When active chi (yang) is in balance with passive chi (yin), harmony exists and life could not be better. Happiness abounds, family love thrives, good health is abundant, and learning comes fast and easy.

Some people consider Feng Shui an environmental science because it involves manipulating the physical elements of a space to create a positive psychological effect. Move furniture, add colors and objects, open pathways, circulate fresh air—when you mindfully alter the flow of energy in your nursery you can't help but affect how your baby feels. Done wisely, you can create a harmonious atmosphere that fosters all aspects of development and success.

Paint a wall to heighten self-confidence, hang a picture to tighten family bonds, select furniture that fosters kindness, put a bookcase where it can inspire a lifelong love of learning. Even the simple act of throwing open your nursery window and letting your baby hear the

birds can have a profound effect on the person your baby will become.

Nursery Feng Shui isn't difficult, and it need not cost a lot of money (cleaning, for instance, is one of Feng Shui's most powerful tools yet it costs nothing but your time). All it requires is a desire to affect positive change and a little intuitive creativity (which, as parents, by necessity, you already have).

So if you're planning to have a baby, preparing to have a baby, or already have a baby, this book is for you. Sit down, browse through its pages, and let your imagination take flight. Trust yourself to know what's right, and take time to enjoy the Feng Shui process. The more love you put into creating a positive nursery environment, the more richly rewarded your baby will be—now and for the rest of his or her life.

A PRIMER IN YIN AND YANG

Healthy babies are full of energy, which makes them naturally yang. To enhance their natural energy and ensure healthy growth, make sure the energy of their nursery leans slightly more toward yang than yin. Here are a few points to consider:

The brighter the natural light the better—avoid trees outside windows.

- Deep colors are generally preferable to pale colors.

- Circles and squares are generally preferable to stripes, triangles, and rectangles.

- Tall furniture is more nursery-appropriate than low furniture.

- Active pictures (a kangaroo jumping rope) are preferable to inactive pictures (a bunny sleeping).

CONFIDENCE

No matter where you place a crib or bassinet, make sure one edge is flush against a wall. This will lend support for healthy development and confidence.

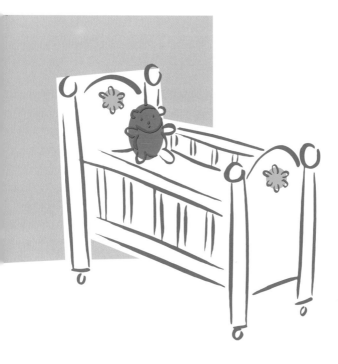

THE IDEAL PLACE FOR A CRIB

According to the principles of Feng Shui, the ideal place to put a crib is at a diagonal to the door with its headboard against a wall. In this way your baby is safe from any negative chi that might seep through the door and is protected by the strength of a solid wall.

NORTH

To help calm overly active babies,
position their cribs so their heads
are to the north. You may not be
able to quiet their days, but it will
help fill their nights with tranquillity.

WIND CHIMES

Instead of hanging a traditional mobile, hang metallic wind chimes instead. Look for those that ring easily in a gentle breeze, and hang them near a window. Their tinkling sound can help stimulate nursery chi while their shifting reflections can stimulate your baby's curiosity.

USE COLOR TO BALANCE TEMPERAMENT

What color you paint your nursery can have a profound effect on your baby's temperament. Use the suggestions on the following pages to help balance your baby's chi and bring harmony to your family life.

Red inspires activity. Fiery red can spark a desire to learn, but too much can cause sleeplessness. Paint one wall red if your baby is shy or reluctant. Pink shades promote curiosity.

Orange promotes family bonds. It's an especially useful color if yours is a blended family. Avoid orange if your baby is overly sensitive—orange encourages emotional attachments and can increase separation anxiety.

Yellow encourages cheerfulness. Earthy yellow is the color of life-giving sunlight—use it to enliven a quiet baby, but avoid it if your baby is colicky. Yellow's energy is pointed and sharp and may increase aggravation.

Green inspires mental development. Its vibrant energy is that of wood, and it instills babies with a desire to learn and grow. But too much green can be overstimulating and lead an active baby to exhaustion.

Blue induces calm. Its water energy is most useful in helping soothe colicky or anxious babies, but too much blue can dull curiosity and slow active development. Turquoise heightens self-confidence.

Violet encourages independence. Violet is ideal for a physically or emotionally challenged baby because it promotes introspection and steadfastness. Avoid violet if your baby is shy.

THE MAGIC OF SEA SALT

Sea salt tends to wick excess energy from a room the same way table salt absorbs moisture. To calm overactive nursery chi and help your baby sleep soundly, keep a bowl of sea salt on the dresser.

NOT THE TIME TO CLEAN

Avoid cleaning the nursery before nap or bedtime. Though your intentions may be noble, a good cleaning often whips dust into the air and leaves behind unnatural scents that disturb tranquil chi. The most auspicious time to clean the nursery is just after your baby wakes up.

THE CHI OF FABRIC

When shopping for crib sheets, bumpers, comforters, and blankets, choose fabrics that are smooth but not silky. Smooth textures (cotton, cotton knits, velvet) are naturally yin and promote calm, quiet, and sleep. Silky textures (polyester, silk, satin) are yang and tend to foster excitement and action—emotions more suited for playtime.

WINDOWS

Never place a crib under a window. The active in-and-out flow of chi through a window can make your baby jumpy and may prohibit deep sleep.

THE CHI OF WINDOW COVERINGS

Never mind what those trendy magazines advise—
the best window treatments for a nursery are those
old-fashioned fabric blinds. During the night they
block light but allow chi to seep through. During
the day they can be rolled up to expose the whole
window, allowing a maximum circulation of energy.

BEWARE OF BEAMS

Open beams may be a charming feature but when it comes to sound sleep they're a nightmare. Ceiling beams create a downward draft of chi, wreaking havoc on the tranquillity of anyone below. If your nursery has a beamed ceiling, place your baby's crib or bassinet between the beams, not under them.

Toys are an essential part of any nursery, even if your baby's too young to interact with them. Because each toy has its own type of energy, it can be used in various combinations to affect the chi of the room. Decorating with toys can be especially useful for moody babies—they can easily be changed to reinforce or counteract the day's (or hour's) prevailing emotion.

Use yang toys to stimulate and excite:

- Activity centers and gyms
- Talking games
- Swings and jumpers
- Pull toys

Use yin toys to calm and soothe:

- Stacking toys
- Books and puzzles
- Music boxes
- Stuffed animals

THE WONDER OF WATER

Water features are said to infuse a room with luck, especially when placed in the northeast of a room (out of your baby's reach, of course!). Consider a goldfish bowl, a tabletop fountain, or something from the water, like a conch shell.

ROCKING CHAIR CHI

No nursery would be complete without the magic of a rocking chair (or a modern rocker-glider). The most harmonious are those made of natural materials like wood and wicker. If you prefer the upholstered variety, choose one with large cushions and rectangular-patterned fabric—two yin qualities that invite relaxation.

FAVORABLE SEATING

The best place to put a rocking chair in your nursery is in the north, facing south. North is the direction of peace and tranquillity; facing south will inspire mental development. Next best would be southwest facing northeast. These are the directions of family harmony and steady progress.

According to ancient Chinese legend, each calendar year is ruled by an animal who shares its characteristics with babies born during its reign. To celebrate and strengthen your baby's emerging personality, keep a symbol of his or her ruling animal in the nursery—a stuffed animal, a pillow, artwork, a mural, even something as small as a decorative light switch plate.

2004 Year of the Monkey:
Monkeys are creative, friendly, clever.
2005 Year of the Rooster:
Roosters are talented, eager, capable.
2006 Year of the Dog:
Dogs are faithful, honest, compassionate.
2007 Year of the Pig:
Pigs are courageous, peaceful, loving.
2008 Year of the Rat:
Rats are loyal, charming, intelligent.
2009 Year of the Ox:
Oxen are patient, strong, self-reliant.

2010 Year of the Tiger:

Tigers are adventurous, imaginative, ambitious.

2011 Year of the Hare:

Hares are generous, intuitive, optimistic.

2012 Year of the Dragon:

Dragons are confident, lucky, energetic.

2013 Year of the Snake:

Snakes are intellectual, curious, wise.

2014 Year of the Horse:

Horses are social, industrious, expressive.

2015 Year of the Goat:

Goats are sincere, artistic, affectionate.

GROWING CREATIVITY

Childhood is a time of curiosity and wonder. That is, after all, how we learn. To enhance your baby's natural curiosity, create a play area in the west side of the nursery. Activity gyms, mirrors, and baby swings should all be available here. West is the direction of creativity and active play here can help sharpen the mind.

PUT A LID ON IT

Always keep the lid on the diaper pail! Not only will your nursery smell sweeter, but it will also help keep healthy chi from going down the drain.

LUCKY ORANGE

The scent of orange is said to be lucky. Fortunately, it also masks odors. A few drops of orange oil inside your diaper pail can make your baby lucky in two ways.

WALLPAPER

The best patterns for nursery fabric and wallpaper are those with a vertical repeat, like stripes. They echo a child's upward growth and can instill a passion for life.

NOTHING OVER, NOTHING UNDER

The more room chi has to circulate around a crib, the healthier and more restorative its energy will be. To ensure good overall health and development, don't hang anything over a crib and never store anything below.

THE IMPORTANCE OF BOOKS

No baby is too young for books and no nursery should be without a bookshelf. The ideal bookshelf is made of wood (to support growth), is tall (to incite a passion for learning), and is on the east side of the nursery (the direction of new beginnings). Be sure to keep it dust- and clutter-free.

SIBLING HARMONY

If you have twins (or triplets, or more) align their cribs so they sleep in the same direction to inspire a harmonious relationship between them. Aligning cribs with the beds of older siblings works well for family harmony, too.

CALMING COLIC

Colicky babies can try the patience of even the calmest parent on earth. To help calm your rattled nerves and fortify your spirit, try cuddling your baby in the north facing south. This is the direction of inner peace looking toward new ideas.

LOCATION IS EVERYTHING

If you have a choice of which room to use as a nursery, consider the location very carefully. Different areas of a home affect different energies and in turn can influence your baby in many different ways. The best locations to consider are:

East. This is the direction of new beginnings, youth, growth, and development. Its chi is typically active and exciting. If you find its activity disturbs your baby's sleep, calm it by decorating with soft shades of blue.

Southeast. This is the direction of creativity, communication, and action. Like the east, its chi encourages growth but at a slightly slower pace. A nursery here can provide a harmonious atmosphere for both play and rest.

West. This is the direction of calm and contentment, which makes it ideal for sleep. Its chi is settled and peaceful but still playful enough for learning. If you find its energy is too lethargic, decorate with bright colors, a water feature, crystals, or a bell.

FEED THE FLOW

Crystals, wind chimes, and mirrors in a nursery all achieve the same effect: They redirect the stream of chi and keep positive energy flowing freely.

THE MAGIC OF MIRRORS

Mirrors have many uses in Feng Shui and can be
especially useful in a nursery: They enhance natural
light, circulate positive chi, and help stimulate your
baby's social development. The best mirrors are those
within a baby's field of vision (low on the wall is ideal)
and are large enough to reflect their whole head. In
Feng Shui, reflections signify abundance—if you can
position your nursery mirror so it also reflects you,
your baby will feel twice as loved.

CEILING FANS

Even if you live in a temperate climate you'd be wise to consider installing a ceiling fan in your nursery. Set it so the blades rotate counterclockwise. An upward draft of air strengthens the chi of the room.

LIGHTING

The most auspicious lamp for a nursery is one that casts light directly upward so it's reflected back down into the room. You may need to resist those darling Mother Goose figurines and opt for something more mature, but the benefits will be well worth it. Like light from the sun, soft lighting that falls from above nourishes, soothes, and enlivens.

THE PARADOX OF SKYLIGHTS

A preexisting skylight in a nursery is an auspicious and positive feature. Like a window, it's a portal for chi to flow in and out of, infusing the room with life. But it's considered unlucky to add a skylight to a nursery where one didn't exist before. Cutting into a home's roof is like cutting into a body—it can expose your baby to all kinds of ills. It's better to leave the nursery roof untouched and enhance natural light with mirrors.

FURNISHING AND THE FIVE ELEMENTS

Furniture and accessories are much more than decorations—each corresponds to a different earthly element and can affect a room's energy in a different way. Use them to influence your baby's development by mixing and matching different types.

- Wood, wicker, and bamboo are filled with wood energy and promote kindness.

- Plastic is filled with fire energy and can encourage expression.

- Plaster, clay, and brick are filled with earth energy and can inspire reliability.

- Metal is filled with metal energy and can promote leadership.

- Glass is filled with water energy and can encourage wisdom.

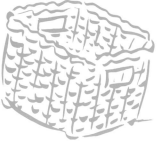

SYMBOLS OF THE FIVE ELEMENTS

Light is a symbol of the element fire, which influences emotions. To help your baby grow up strong and passionate, keep a night light on in the nursery.

Bamboo is a symbol of the element wood, which influences faith. To help your baby develop confidence and trust, hang a bamboo flute on the wall.

Clay and soil are symbols of the element earth, which influences security. To help your baby grow up secure and well grounded, keep a clay-potted plant on a shelf.

Silver is a symbol of the element metal, which influences ambition. To help your baby become a natural leader, keep a silver Tooth Fairy box on the dresser.

Fish and glass are symbols of the element water, which influences wisdom. To help your baby grow up tranquil and accepting, keep a small fishbowl high out of reach.

CUT OUT CUTTING CHI

Beware of furnishings with sharp or pointed edges.
Not only do they pose a physical danger to your
baby, but they're dangerous in Feng Shui terms as
well. Sharp edges thrust chi outward with such
force it "cuts" right through a room's positive chi.
Cutting chi is highly destructive and should be
avoided at all costs.

CUTTING CHI REMEDIES

If you simply cannot avoid sharp edges in a nursery, soften their cutting chi by covering them. Drape cloths or runners over the edges of tables; let the tendrils of bushy, vining plants droop over dressers and shelves.

ENHANCING THE CHI OF WOOD

Because wood is the symbol of life and growth, it's the most recommended material for nursery furnishings. But wood doesn't need to remain natural—in fact, painting wood can enhance its chi. Choose blue or green to increase vitality, yellow to enhance power, pink to supplement social development, red to grow up lucky, or purple to grow up wise.

BALANCING ACT

Nurseries are contradictory rooms—they're used for both sleep and play—which can make them difficult to harmonize. Add to that your baby's unpredictable moods, and harmony may seem impossible. It's not! The secret is keeping a few simple objects on hand to tip energy one way or another, then tuck away for next time.

Yang (active) objects include:

- Circles, octagons, and squares (think marbles, bells, boxes)

- Red and orange ornaments

- Hard surfaces like marble, stone, and glass

Yin (quiet) objects include:

- Rectangles, thin and wavy shapes (think baskets, trays, figurines)

- Blue and green ornaments

- Soft surfaces like fabric, wicker, and wood

ABOVE ALL ELSE, DECLUTTER

If you only have time to do one thing to your nursery, make it clutter-free! Clutter acts like a beaver's dam, stopping the flow of chi and causing it to stagnate. The result is an atmosphere that inhibits healthy growth. At the end of every day, declutter! Put away those toys! Stack those diapers! Shelve those books! And for heaven's sake, remember that the rocking chair was not intended to hold blankets and clothes! The few minutes you spend picking up the nursery can give your baby days of peace.

CLOSET CHI

Just because you can't see it doesn't mean it's not there. Dark and cluttered closets are havens for stagnant chi. Next time you clean the nursery, clean the closet, too!

STROLLERS

Strollers and baby carriages are like cars. If they must be stored in the nursery, park them in the closet.

THE NINE AREAS OF INFLUENCE

According to the principles of Feng Shui, every room has nine areas of influence. Energizing one area (like wealth) is said to heighten its influence on your life (to help you find abundance). To make sure that your baby grows up well balanced, it's a good idea to energize all nine areas equally.

Relationships

The southwest area of your nursery influences relationships. To strengthen the bond your baby has with you, keep this area neat and clean. A cozy chair here where the two of you can snuggle can help secure that very special connection.

Recognition

The south part of your nursery is the area of recognition. To help your baby feel recognized and celebrated, keep some newborn mementos here, like a framed hand or footprint, a first lock of hair, or a photograph of your baby just minutes old.

Wealth

The southeast area of your nursery influences wealth. To ensure your baby has a wealth of love all his or her life, keep something gold here. Goldfish are a perfect choice (real or ornamental) but so is a gold-toned piggy bank, a golden sun, gold stars, or a glowing moon.

Family

The east part of your nursery is the area of family and heritage. Family photos and heirlooms here will help strengthen your baby's family ties. This is also the place to display cultural objects so your baby feels proud of his or her heritage.

Knowledge

The northeast area of your nursery influences knowledge. To help your baby acquire a love of learning, keep this area filled with books—neatly shelved on a dust-free bookcase, of course.

Career

The north part of your nursery influences career. Since it's a baby's job to learn about the world, you can help by keeping educational toys here—mirrors, rattles, play gyms, stacking toys, and later, puzzles.

Helpful People

The northwest corner of your nursery is the area of helpful people. This is an especially important area to pay close attention to if your baby spends time with a caregiver. Help fortify that bond by keeping a photo of your caregiver here—or a special gift from the caregiver to your baby.

Creativity

The west part of your nursery is the area of creativity. Ample floor play here can help your baby develop a sense of self-reliance and creative thinking skills. Later, keep all exploratory and creative toys here, like Play-Doh, crayons, paint, and puppets.

Good Health

The center of your nursery is the area of good health. To help your baby grow up strong and healthy, make sure the center of your nursery is empty. The more freedom of movement chi has here, the more positive and uplifting its energy will be.

NEGATIVE SPACE

In Feng Shui terms, less is often a whole lot more. Keep nursery furnishings to a minimum and have only what you need. Likewise, nursery walls should be mostly bare. The more space you give chi to roam, the happier, healthier, and luckier your baby will be.

RING OUT THE OLD

Before converting an old room into a nursery, it's a good idea to ring out negative chi. Walk slowly around the room ringing a soft-sounding bell.

THE SWEETEST SOUNDS

Next to your voice, the sweetest sound a baby can hear is the soothing sound of nature. Throw open those windows and let your baby hear the birds! Welcome the sound of the wind! On cold nights and rainy days, try playing a nature CD.

THE RULE OF FOUR

When it comes to electronic devices in a nursery, a good number to remember is four. Try to have no more than four devices (a baby monitor, a night light, a lamp, a CD player) and keep them at least four feet from the crib. Electromagnetic fields can greatly disturb an environment, so the fewer and farther from your baby the better.

THE FAMILY BED

If your baby sleeps in a family bed, you'd be wise to sleep with your head pointing either east or southwest. East is the direction of the rising sun, growth, and all possibilities. Southwest is the direction of family harmony, steady progress, and inner peace.

STAIRWAY CHI

Stairways are to the flow of chi what a waterfall is to a river. The longer and steeper the drop, the faster the energy flows. If your nursery is at the top of a stairway, it could be draining of healthy chi; if it's at the bottom, it could be drowning under too much. To slow the flow of chi and recirculate energy upward, hang a mirror at the bottom of the stairway reflecting the top step.

BEHIND CLOSED DOORS

It's an age-old tenet of Feng Shui that bedroom doors should be closed when sleeping. This is true of nurseries also, although it might make some parents uneasy. If you fall into that category, a high-quality baby monitor would be a worthy investment.

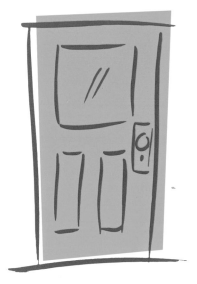

NURSING MOMS

Babies aren't the only ones who require an atmosphere of peace and harmony. Nursing mothers need one, too. When you decorate the nursery, put yourself in the picture! Keep a small table next to a comfortable rocker or glider and on it put fresh flowers, something sentimental, and *your* favorite (quiet) CD.

MOBILES

Contrary to the Western way of thinking, you should never hang a mobile directly over a crib or changing table. Its chi can be dangerously heavy.

ELEMENTAL ARTWORK

Few things set the tone of a room more than artwork. In the nursery, choose your artwork wisely.
For a perfectly harmonious atmosphere, hang five
separate pieces, each representing a different
earth element. Try stars for fire, a tree for wood,
dolphins or snowmen for water, a rocket for metal,
and a bunny for earth.

BLACK AND WHITE

Black-and-white mobiles, wallpaper, pictures, and toys are ideal ornaments for a nursery. Not only does their high visual contrast help babies learn about the physical world, they're also a perfect blend of yin and yang.

HOW TO NEUTRALIZE PLASTIC

Plastic is unavoidable in a modern nursery, but its chi is not always favorable. To neutralize its negative energy, store plastics in natural fiber containers. Try a wicker basket for diapers, a wooden box for toiletries and pacifiers, and a rattan planter for diaper wipes. Get creative! Have fun! Your baby will be healthier for it.

THIS BOOK WAS DESIGNED
AND TYPESET IN UNIVERS
BY ANN ZIPKIN OF ANN-DESIGN,
KATONAH, NEW YORK.